ORCA
FOOTPRINTS

Trash Talk

MOVING TOWARD A ZERO-WASTE WORLD

MICHELLE MULDER

ORCA BOOK PUBLISHERS

For Susan

The world's oceans are swirling with garbage,
and Boyan Slat plans to clean them up. THEOCEANCLEANUP.COM

Library and Archives Canada Cataloguing in Publication

Mulder, Michelle, 1976–, author
Trash talk : moving toward a zero-waste world / Michelle Mulder.
(Orca footprints)

Includes index.
Issued in print and electronic formats.
ISBN 978-1-4598-0692-4 (bound).—ISBN 978-1-4598-0693-1(pdf).—
ISBN 978-1-4598-0694-8 (epub)

1. Refuse and refuse disposal—Juvenile literature.
I. Title. II. Series: Orca footprints

TD792.M84 2015   j363.72'8   c2014-906687-2
                        c2014-906688-0

First published in the United States, 2015
Library of Congress Control Number: 2014952068

Summary: People all over the world are working to keep our planet
from drowning in a sea of garbage.

*Orca Book Publishers is dedicated to preserving the environment and has
printed this book on Forest Stewardship Council® certified paper.*

Orca Book Publishers gratefully acknowledges the support for
its publishing programs provided by the following agencies:
the Government of Canada through the Canada Book Fund and the
Canada Council for the Arts, and the Province of British Columbia
through the BC Arts Council and the Book Publishing Tax Credit.

Cover images by Getty Images and Gavin Swan/Two Hands Project
Back cover images (top left to right): Dreamstime, Artechstudios.ca,
Žiga Šmidovnik, (bottom left to right): Peter Bennett,
Landfillharmonicmovie.com, Amy Hansen

Design and production by Teresa Bubela and Jenn Playford

ORCA BOOK PUBLISHERS   ORCA BOOK PUBLISHERS
PO Box 5626, STN. B   PO Box 468
Victoria, BC Canada   Custer, WA USA
V8R 6S4   98240-0468

www.orcabook.com
Printed and bound in Canada.

18 17 16 15 • 4 3 2 1

Contents

CHAPTER ONE:
A WEALTH OF WASTE

CHAPTER TWO:
HEAPS OF POSSIBILITIES

CHAPTER THREE:
THE GREAT DUMPSTER DIVE

CHAPTER FOUR:
NO GARBAGE HERE

Introduction

We found this dresser on a sidewalk just a few blocks from home. (Thank goodness it was close by. It was heavy!) GASTÓN CASTAÑO

Have you ever found treasure in a trash bin? It's a risky activity, of course. Garbage is smelly, germy and often dangerous. That's why, when I was twenty, I didn't tell my parents I'd started Dumpster diving.

I lived in a building with hundreds of other university students. In April, most of us moved away for the summer, and whatever didn't fit into suitcases got tossed. On my first Dumpster dive, I found seven novels, a set of speakers, a frying pan and an unopened box of Earl Grey tea—all perfectly good. I've been thinking about trash ever since.

What makes something garbage? I used to think trash was something no one could use anymore. Boy, was I wrong. Wait until you see how people use garbage! In Paraguay, old water pipes become saxophones. In Haiti, worn-out tires turn into house walls. Around the world, fishermen collect abandoned fishing nets to be made into carpets for office buildings. With some creative thinking, garbage doesn't have to exist at all. Want to see what that would look like? Grab a cloth bag and a reusable water bottle and follow me!

Beware the scary waste monster! This awareness-raising sculpture spreads its plastic tentacles through the streets of Ljubljana, Slovenia. ŽIGA ŠMIDOVNIK

Take in the Trash!

My daughter loves shouting "Free pile!" from her seat on our bicycle. Where we live in Victoria, British Columbia, people often leave unwanted items on the side of the road with a sign saying Free. Maia and I screech to a stop and hop down to investigate. So far, her favorite find has been a big teddy bear in perfect condition, but we've taken home everything from plates to plants to furniture.

My family always looks out for free piles on weekend bike rides. MICHELLE MULDER

CHAPTER ONE

A Wealth of Waste

A MYSTERIOUS NEW INVENTION

What is garbage anyway?

Picture an empty yogurt container. It could be trash. But it could also become a pencil holder or a flower vase or a container for picking blackberries. An item only becomes trash when we decide that it's no longer useful for anything else. People have always tossed trash, but a few human inventions have really made it pile up.

INTO THE BUSH

If you were living hundreds of thousands of years ago, you might have woken up each morning in a cave. Breakfast would be the roasted leg of a wild bird you had hunted the day before. When your belly is full, you look down at the bone in your hand. What could you use it for? Should you tie your hair around it to keep loose strands out of your face? Or should you dip the bone in ash and use it to draw pictures on the wall? Then again, maybe it could be a piece for a new game to play with the other kids.

Who says boots are only for feet? Creative container gardening turns broken boots into fancy flowerpots. POOPIX/ISTOCK.COM

Just as you're imagining the rules of your new game, your mother grunts at you. It's time to feed the fire, pick the bugs out of your little brother's hair and find some berries for lunch. You toss the bone into the bush until later. If you forget about it, nature will turn it into soil again (more about that in Chapter Two). But chances are you'll remember. Stores haven't been invented yet, and if you want a hair clip or a pencil or a toy, you've got to make it yourself.

RUBBISH, RATS AND RASHES

Back in the days of living in caves, people traveled around a lot, following their food with the changes of the seasons. Then, about 12,000 years ago, people in the Near East (western Asia) started farming. For the first time ever, people began living in one place all year round. Cities formed, and city dwellers did what they'd done in the countryside: they threw what they didn't want out the window. But this time, their chicken bones and carrot tops didn't land in the bush. They landed in the street.

Each civilization had its own ideas about what to do with garbage. The Minoan people (who lived on the island of Crete about 5,000 years ago) tossed their trash in a pit outside their settlement and covered it over with dirt to keep down the smell. Two thousand years ago, the Chinese composted food scraps and recycled metals like bronze into new tools. Around the same time, on the other side of the planet, the Mayans of Central America were recycling some of their garbage and burying or burning the rest. Mostly, though, for thousands of years, trash landed in the street.

In 1280, the citizens of London, England, were told to stop tossing waste out the window. No one suggested anywhere else to put the trash, though, so most people ignored the new rule. Cats, dogs, pigs, rats, mice, bugs and bacteria feasted on the stuff in the streets. Not long afterward, in Paris, France,

For hundreds of years, garbage filled the streets of London. Evening strolls were more enjoyable if you held your nose! LEBRECHT MUSIC & ARTS

Ancient Minoans buried trash in pits like this one. YVAN POINTURIER

TRASH FACT: Five thousand years ago, in the city of Troy (in what is now Turkey), people cleaned up the streets by covering trash with dirt and laying down new paving stones. All that garbage meant streets became 1.5 meters (5 feet) higher every century.

the city's defenders complained that big piles of trash at the city gates blocked their view of invaders. Worried about the safety of their city, people cleared the gates but left rubbish in the rest of the streets. The rubbish attracted rats, which had fleas, which carried a disease called the bubonic plague. Between 1347 and 1352, one-third to one-half of Europe's population died of this disease.

FULL STEAM AHEAD!

Hundreds of years ago, people made everything by hand. On farms, men built their own houses, made their own furniture and grew their own food. Women cooked all the meals and made sheets, blankets, curtains and clothes for the entire family. (They made their own fabric by weaving plant fibers like flax or cotton into cloth.) All of these activities took a long time.

Then in 1769, a Scottish man named James Watt invented a machine that changed everything—the steam engine. When businessmen discovered that steam engines could power machines for weaving and sewing, they built clothing factories all over Europe. People loved the idea of buying inexpensive, factory-made clothes in a store instead of spending days making them at home.

Of course, all these factories needed people to work in them. Factory owners offered regular work and regular paychecks. And for many farmers, the security of factory work seemed like a great deal.

In 1801, P.J. Loutherbourg painted Ironbridge, England, as a smoke-filled city. As the Industrial Revolution spread across Europe, so did industrial pollution.
P.J. LOUTHERBOURG/WIKIPEDIA.ORG

A CITY LIFE FOR ME

Picture yourself living on a farm hundreds of years ago. Every day you and your parents work from sunrise to sunset, growing potatoes, cabbages, and other vegetables to sell at the market. Some years you make enough money to survive. Other years storms or disease destroy all your crops, and you eat turnip soup for months on end. Then a neighbor tells your dad about a factory in the city where adults and kids can get well-paying jobs with regular paychecks. Your family could eat well all year round without ever having to worry about weather or plant diseases.

In the late 1700s, thousands of people moved from the countryside to work in factories. Whole families worked long hours in dark, noisy, dangerous buildings but made enough money to buy food and clothing. Sometimes they had cash left over for furniture, blankets and toys too. And that was good because city families had far less time to make or fix belongings. Eventually, people began to throw away broken things and buy new ones instead.

The more factories opened, the more people came to live in cities. People bought more products than ever before, and all this buying produced more trash.

In London in the 1800s, children earned a few coins by sweeping garbage away from doorways. VICTORIAN PICTURE LIBRARY

TRASH FACT: In the 1860s, in New York City, local coffee companies made a cheap, coffee-like drink by roasting and grinding a blend of chicory root and street sweepings. Now that's recycling at its most disgusting!

Take in the Trash!

When I was nineteen, I spent a summer in a rural village in the Dominican Republic. I barely used a trash can the whole time, partly because I didn't buy much. Buying less meant I didn't generate as much trash. Also, any trash that I did produce—like an empty water bottle, for example—was useful to someone else. In fact, I don't remember seeing any garbage anywhere the whole summer I was there!

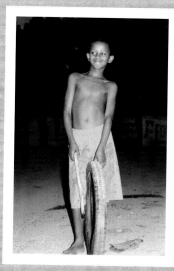

This boy in the Dominican Republic turned a bicycle tire and a stick into a running and balancing game.
MICHELLE MULDER

On strike! In 1911, New York City garbage collectors demanded to work in daylight. Nighttime collection was too dangerous.
SKU: L-21272/BAINS NEWS SERVICE

WHERE DO WE PUT IT ALL?

Imagine stepping out of your door into a pile of garbage. Off to the left, you hear a pig snuffling around, eating last night's leftovers. To your right, a man with a cart is collecting rags and bottles to sell to factories (or maybe bits of rotting food scraps, stale bread, dead cats, rats and puppies to sell to the sausage maker. *Blech!*) This is New York City in 1850, a city so stinky that sailors could smell it almost ten kilometers (six miles) out to sea.

Around this time, scientists throughout Europe were learning that germs live in garbage and spread disease. Several cities around the world, including New York, banned tossing trash into the streets and instead began to organize regular garbage collection from people's homes and businesses. In some places, people sorted through the garbage, sent food scraps to "piggeries," where seventy-five pigs could eat about 900 kilograms (almost 1 ton) of food scraps per day, and either tossed leftover trash into a big pit or burned it and used the ash for fertilizer.

TRASH FACT: In Britain in the 1800s, "toshers" made a living by scavenging and reselling coins, bits of metal, ropes, and even jewelry that they found by poking through —*blech*—the sewers!

Then in 1912, in England, people developed a "new" way to deal with trash—new because no one recalled that the Minoans had done the same thing 5,000 years earlier. They dug a pit, tossed in the garbage, compacted it, and covered it regularly with dirt to keep it from blowing away and to stop the stench from attracting animals. This kind of pit was known as a sanitary landfill, and within a few decades, cities around the world were building them.

PLASTIC DREAMS

These days we talk a lot about reducing, reusing and recycling because it's good for the Earth. Did you know that in the 1940s, many people reduced, reused and recycled because it was good for...a war?

Every country involved in the Second World War used many resources to make weapons and all the other items needed for the war effort. Countries asked their citizens to donate scrap paper, metal, cooking fat and all sorts of other materials to make everything from bullets to bombs. Then factory owners learned about a material that British inventor Alexander Parkes had created in 1862. Factories could make it themselves very cheaply, and they'd never have to wait for donations of other materials again. Before long, factories were making helmet liners, cockpit windows, goggles and parts for the atomic bomb with this amazing new material: plastic.

NO MORE DISHWASHING!

But what do you do with a helmet-liner factory after the war is over? If you're like many businessmen of the 1940s and '50s, you think up another plastic product that people might want. And then you make sure they hear about it!

Bottles, rags and food scraps from "the dumps" could earn these boys in Boston, Massachussetts, a good bit of cash.
LEWIS HINE/WIKIMEDIA COMMONS

STILL MORE
PAPER RAGS BONES
WANTED FOR SALVAGE

During World War II, scrap paper, cloth and bones weren't garbage—they were valuable resources used to make war equipment.
CONRAD POIRIER/WIKIMEDIA COMMONS

By using plastic, factories could make more products faster than ever before. At the same time, television had been invented, so manufacturers had a way to tell people about new products. One commercial in the United States showed a miserable housewife washing dishes and dreaming of a happier life. When her husband gives her a stack of disposable dishes, she dances happily across the screen, throwing plates, cutlery, cups, napkins, tablecloth and leftovers into the trash, and gets ready to enjoy the rest of her day.

Disposable everything seemed to be the key to happiness. After years of having to reduce, reuse and recycle to win the war, many people were thrilled to be able to buy things, throw them away and then buy more.

Take in the Trash!

I love living by the ocean, walking along the shore and watching sunlight glisten on the water. But a few decades ago, here in Victoria, BC, my time on the beach would have been very different. From 1908 to 1958, city workers loaded all of Victoria's garbage onto barges and dumped it in the ocean. The tide washed it back to shore, though, and picnickers brought rakes to clear places to sit on the sand! I'm glad I've never had to pack a rake for my seaside lunches.

All year round, my family heads to the beach on sunny days. PILAR ROQUENI

BACK TO NATURE

Not everyone is thrilled with the "disposable" lifestyle though. Since the Industrial Revolution (when factories began belching black smoke into Earth's air and pouring waste into the water), many have worried about how human activities harm the planet.

The environmental movement got stronger and stronger as the years went by and the trash piled higher. These days, many people are asking themselves if "disposable" is really so convenient after all. Where are we going to put all our trash, and what's it doing to our environment?

Something only becomes trash when we decide it's not useful anymore. So what if we start looking at what we have and using it instead of throwing it away? Our banana peels become compost to feed the soil. Our yogurt containers become pots to grow flowers. Our blue jeans become housing insulation. With creative thinking, stuff we once threw away can become a collection of valuable resources, just waiting to be harvested. After all, that's how the world has worked since long before humans walked the Earth.

Erek Hansen collects worn-out jeans. He's collected thousands—not to wear, but to insulate houses for people in need.
AMY HANSEN

Every year, on April 22, people around the world celebrate Earth Day. These folks are sharing their thoughts in Vancouver, British Columbia. HOWESJWE/DREAMSTIME.COM

CHAPTER TWO

Heaps of Possibilities

THE DIRT ON TRASH

The tiny creatures in compost make rich soil that grows great veggies!
ALLKINDZA/ISTOCK.COM

Humans have always generated garbage, whether it's a chewed-on leg bone or a broken cell phone. And until not so long ago, most of our trash eventually turned into soil.

How does trash become dirt? Think back to the bone you threw out when you were a cavekid in Chapter One. If you left it in the bush, a vulture might pick off any remaining meat. Then tiny creatures called *microorganisms* would gather on the surface of the bone and eat away at it. After many years, microorganisms would eventually eat the entire bone, returning its nutrients to the soil. Plants absorb those nutrients, and animals feed on the plants. Later, those animals die, and the cycle begins again.

Anything that these microorganisms can break down into soil is called *biodegradable*. Whether it's a bone, a dead body, poop or potato peels, all biodegradable materials are food for microorganisms. What one creature doesn't need anymore, another uses as food. Nothing is wasted. This brilliant system has allowed nature to thrive since life on Earth began, billions of years ago.

Dig in! This school compost pile in Los Angeles, California, will help students grow plenty of nutritious food. PETER BENNETT

NO DIRT

Have you ever tried to make a knife out of chicken parts or a shovel out of, say, cabbage leaves? Early people made tools out of bones, but as soon as they learned how to use a harder material, they did.

People began making stone tools about 12,000 years ago, and metal ones about 5,300 years ago. These were the first human-made items that nature's recycling system couldn't munch into dirt. Because they were difficult to make, these tools were precious objects. Parents passed them on to their children, and if a tool broke, the owner repaired or remade it. Most people would never have dreamed of throwing out a tool. This was how the world worked for thousands of years.

When factories began making products faster and more cheaply than ever before, tools and other items didn't seem so precious anymore. And after World War II, plastic products were almost always cheaper to replace than to repair. More and more items became trash.

TRASH FACT: Microorganisms need oxygen to break down biodegradable items quickly. In landfills, scientists have dug up fifty-year-old newspapers and twenty-five-year-old hot dogs, corncobs and grapes, all looking much as they did the day people threw them away!

Seabirds, especially young ones, often mistake plastic for food.
CHRIS JORDAN/WIKIMEDIA.ORG

Today, our planet is home to seven times as many people as in 1800. Most of us are producing mounds of garbage every year, and a lot of it isn't biodegradable. For the first time since life on Earth began, one species—the human being—is creating items that no one else can use. And wherever we look, waste is piling up.

RUBBER DUCKY AT SEA

Picture yourself on a sailboat north of Hawaii. The sun shines above you, and the ocean glistens as far as you can see. For a moment, you imagine yourself and your family as the only humans on Earth. Then you spot something yellow floating in the water. It's a rubber ducky. A few meters farther on, you see a candy wrapper and then a toothbrush. You've reached the North Pacific Gyre—also known as the Great Pacific Garbage Patch.

No one put the garbage there on purpose. The world's lakes drain into rivers, which then drain into the oceans. The water carries with it any garbage that crosses its path, and once the garbage reaches the ocean, currents carry it around the world. Eventually, many currents meet in one of the world's five big *gyres* or swirls of water. In the center of the North Pacific Gyre is an expanse of floating plastic that's about six times the size of the United Kingdom. All the gyres have garbage in them, but the North Pacific's has the most. At least one million birds and another 100,000 marine mammals die each year because of the plastic. Often birds or other creatures eat it, thinking that it is food. Plastic fills their stomachs, and they die of starvation. Several species are at risk of extinction because so much plastic is floating around in the oceans. And the oceans aren't the only places where our garbage collects. You can find garbage in forests, grasslands, and even on top of Mount Everest.

Obviously, littering is bad for the environment. But what if everyone put litter in a trash can? Would that solve the problem?

The Two Hands Project website connects people who want to clean the world's beaches. These girls are in Australia.
GAVIN SWAN/TWOHANDSPROJECT

MUNCH, MUNCH, METHANE!

In many parts of the world, the trash in our garbage cans winds up in a landfill. There, big machines squeeze as much garbage into a pit as possible and cover it with dirt. The goal is to use less space and keep down the smell, but compacting and covering the trash causes something else to happen too.

Normally, the microorganisms that break down biodegradable materials use oxygen. When all the air is squeezed out of a landfill, though, the munching microorganisms create a gas called *methane*. Methane catches fire easily, so in many landfills, pipes lead the gas out of the compacted trash to burn in a controlled way. Some landfills burn the gas to get rid of it, and others use the heat from the burning to produce electricity. Either way, when methane burns, it releases carbon dioxide, one of the gases that contributes to global warming. And methane

Many of the items in this landfill could have been reused or recycled.
PHOTOGRAPHERLONDON/DREAMSTIME.COM

Take in the Trash!

Many people try to recycle as much as possible. Tin cans, paper, plastic containers and glass all go into special bins to be remade into new products. In most of the world, though, recycling technology isn't widely available. For example, in Buenos Aires, Argentina, where my husband is from, tin cans go into the trash. The first time my husband saw me wash out a tin can for recycling, he stared at me. "Michelle," he said, as if he were talking to a crazy person, "why are you washing the garbage?"

These days, my husband is an avid tin-can washer and recycler.
MICHELLE MULDER

isn't a landfill's only pollution. Although operators aim to keep the landfill dry, some water filters into the garbage. By the time it reaches the bottom of the landfill, it's full of chemicals. A thick barrier at the bottom is designed to stop this liquid (*leachate*) from escaping into the soil and groundwater. But barriers can leak, and leachate can cause cancer and many other health problems.

HOT STUFF

Not all garbage cans empty into a landfill. In many places, garbage collectors bring trash to an incinerator to be burned. The burning either releases toxic gases into the air, or the incinerator contains the gases and removes the toxins. Some countries, like Sweden, use the heat from burning garbage to make electricity. In fact, Sweden imports garbage from Norway so there is more to burn! After incineration, Sweden sends all the ash, full of toxic chemicals, back to Norway to put into landfills. Even setting fire to garbage doesn't get rid of waste completely.

TRASH FACT:
Seventy percent of the garbage in landfills could have been recycled or reused.

Garbage dumps like this one contaminate air and soil. Engineers design landfills to contain toxins, but leaks and fires still happen. ALEXANDER PODSHIVALOV/DREAMSTIME.COM

Using incinerators also encourages waste. When we think of trash as energy, we might think throwing a slice of bread into the trash can is a good thing because it helps produce electricity. But this way of thinking ignores all the energy that went into making the slice of bread: energy for the farmer's tractor and harvester, energy to run the mill that ground the wheat into flour, energy to drive the flour to the bakery, energy in the bakery to knead and bake the dough, and energy to get the loaf of bread to the store. Throwing away that slice of bread would waste far more energy than an incinerator could ever get from it.

Ugh! No one wants a garbage incinerator in the neighborhood. PANGFOLIO/DREAMSTIME.COM

RECYCLING WORRIES

What do tin cans, newspapers, pop cans and plastic bottles have in common? With proper technology, they're all recyclable. That's good news for landfills, which will be much roomier without tin, paper and certain plastics.

A recycling plant can turn these containers into clothing or other products. OPERATIONSHOOTING88/DREAMSTIME.COM

Even so, sometimes recycling makes environmentalists nervous. First of all, melting down used material to make a new product takes a lot of energy. In most places, the factories that recycle our waste use electricity made with coal. Coal is a fossil fuel, and burning it releases harmful gases that contribute to global warming. Also, many materials—like plastic—can only be recycled a few times. Each time, the product becomes more flimsy and more likely to wind up as garbage eventually. Second, much like burning garbage, recycling often makes people feel better about using something once and tossing it away. But the best thing for the environment is to throw away less in the first place.

Around the world, people are coming up with creative ways to turn garbage into everything from food to furniture. Their goal? To follow nature's example: zero waste.

Recycling this pile of plastic will keep it out of the landfill for a little while longer. ULRICH MUELLER/DREAMSTIME.COM

Take in the Trash!

Have you ever used a garburator? It's an electric gadget under the kitchen sink that mashes up food scraps. A few months ago, my friend Drew decided he didn't want to flush food scraps down the drain anymore. Instead, he'd use his garburator for something better—as a grinder to mash up apples for juicing in an apple press! His kitchen renovation helped him make delicious apple juice for his whole family.

Did you ever imagine that an old sink part could help make apple juice?
STEPHANIE TOLIAS

CHAPTER THREE

The Great Dumpster Dive

LANDFILL OR LUNCH?

If you found a chocolate cake in a Dumpster, would you eat it? And if you found a case of mangoes, a banged-up (but unopened) carton of your favorite juice and a package of cheese, would you bring it all home to stick in your fridge?

A *freegan* would. In many rich countries, freegans find food for their families in supermarket Dumpsters. And it's not because they can't afford to buy food. They simply don't want good food to go to waste, and they know many supermarkets toss whole packages of fruit if one piece is bruised, or a dozen eggs if one is cracked. Freegans find this food, bring it home and eat it themselves or share it with others. One freegan group in New York City offers tours of the city's Dumpsters, followed by a potluck made with delicious found food.

Who would guess this all came from a Dumpster? SIGURDAS/WIKIMEDIA.ORG

Gleaners gather every last bit of goodness from a farmer's field. GARY CEDAR, CROPMOBSTER™ CO-FOUNDER

THE GLEAN TEAM

Experts estimate that we throw away one-third to one-half of all the food we produce on this planet. Not all of it goes into Dumpsters though. Sometimes food goes to waste right in the field where it grew.

Gary Cedar and Nick Papadopoulos started the website Cropmobster™ to change this. Their website connects farmers near San Francisco, California, with local harvesters and hunger-relief programs. Thanks to the Internet and cell phones, a farmer can now decide to thin the crop of, say, tangerines, and within two hours, a few dozen volunteers will show up to pick nearly 800 pounds of fruit for local soup kitchens.

When we throw away food, we waste all the resources that went into creating it. (For example, to raise cattle for beef, a farmer needs land—which means clearing trees—as well as plenty of water and grain or other feed.) The less food we throw away,

TRASH FACT: In a lifetime, the average North American throws out 600 times his or her adult weight in garbage. That means a 68-kilogram (150-pound) adult will create 40,825 kilograms (90,000 pounds) of trash.

After a food market in Milan, Italy, garbage collectors gather discarded food. It might have made a yummy meal a few hours earlier! SHUTTERSTOCK.COM

TRASH FACT: Archaeologists study ancient garbage to understand how past civilizations lived. Scientists who study modern-day trash are called *garbologists*. Our garbage has a whole story to tell about who we are and what's important to us.

the more trees, water and other resources we save. In fact, many environmentalists believe that not wasting food is one of the quickest and most helpful things we can do to save our planet.

TUNEFUL TRASH

For people in many parts of the world, the city dump is home. Forty thousand people live in the city dump in Cairo, Egypt; 10,000 in Managua, Nicaragua; and 12,000 in Manila, the Philippines. They live in tiny shelters built out of garbage, and they earn money by poking through trash, finding reusable materials and selling them.

The dump known as Vertedero Cateura in Paraguay receives 1.4 million kilograms (1,500 tons) of solid waste every day. When Favio Chávez began teaching music to local children in 2006, his classes were so popular that he ran out of instruments for his students. Then a local garbage picker called Nicolás Gómez came to him with an oilcan, a fork, a few bottle caps and an idea. Together they built their first violin. They made a cello out of oilcans, scraps of wood, a spatula and parts of a meat grinder. Water pipes, bottle caps and buttons became flutes and saxophones. X-ray films became drumheads. With all these instruments, they started a children's orchestra—*La Orquesta de Instrumentos Reciclados de Cateura* (the Recycled Orchestra of Cateura, or the Landfill Harmonic)—that now travels around the world. With a little creative thinking and a lot of hard work, other people's trash became a local—and international—treasure.

SITTING ON GARBAGE

Remember the great expanses of plastic in our oceans? What if we could take that litter and do something useful with it?

In 2011, designers Azusa Murakami, Alexander Groves, and Kieren Jones developed the Sea Chair Project. They encouraged

In Paraguay, the Recycled Orchestra of Cateura delights its audiences with instruments made out of garbage. LANDFILLHARMONICMOVIE.COM

Boyan Slat tests equipment he's designed to clean up the world's oceans.

fishermen to fish for plastic and to then use a mini-furnace to mold the plastic into something useful, like a chair. An attached tag shows exactly where in the ocean its plastic came from. Displayed in museums and exhibitions around the world, the Sea Chair Project is raising awareness about our seas, one seat at a time.

Meanwhile, a company called Interface buys abandoned nets that fishermen find floating in the oceans. Factories turn the nets into carpets. After all, why use new materials when you can both help fishermen and save the lives of countless sea creatures?

The plastic in our oceans can be very useful indeed. But collecting it all by boat would take billions of dollars of fuel and thousands of years because most of the plastic is in tiny particles. So, nineteen-year-old Boyan Slat is working on another idea: why not let the ocean do the work for us?

Take in the Trash!

My friend Paul hiked the Appalachian Trail in his twenties. He walked for months, camping at night and occasionally leaving the trail to buy food in a nearby town. At some point, his money was running out, so he and his friends tried Dumpster diving. One store had thrown out many cans of food because the labels had come off. Hungry, the hikers each grabbed a few tins and tried their luck. Some of them had beans for supper and fruit cocktail for dessert, and others wound up with dog food!

Which ones would you choose for your supper? MICHELLE MULDER

He and his team of seventy people are raising money to attach floating structures to the seabed. These structures, designed to trap plastic without harming sea creatures, would wave in the ocean's currents and sweep the plastic to central locations, where it could be collected by a tanker every six weeks. Boyan's team believes they could remove half the plastic in the Great Pacific Garbage Patch in just ten years.

FROM WHEELS TO WALLS

Every year, people throw away millions of tires. Their shape traps air, and the darn things push their way up through landfills, dragging up other stinky trash with them. Some cities keep tires in a separate pile, but those turn into homes for rats and other disease-carrying animals.

The tires and bottles in this Earthship will help keep the house cool in summer and warm in winter. MONA MAKELA/DREAMSTIME.COM

Artist Choi Jeong-Hwa used 1,000 old doors to turn a dull building in Seoul, South Korea, into a masterpiece. CHOI JEONG-HWA/1000 DOOR, MYEONGNYUN 2-GA, 2009

To keep tires out of landfills, some people turn them into planters, swings, footstools or even bike racks. Architect Michael Reynolds uses them to build houses called *Earthships*. First, he and his crew pound as much dirt as possible into dozens of tires. Then they stack them to build sturdy walls. Mr. Reynolds and his crew have built Earthships for people all over the world, often after natural disasters. When an earthquake or tsunami turns a home into a pile of rubble, creative thinking can turn garbage into a home.

A GOOD, WARM BOOK

What do you do with an old book? You could give it to a friend or donate it to a library. But what if you are a library, you're running out of space, and you have thousands of books that no one wants to read anymore?

In 2005, Dalhousie University in Halifax, Nova Scotia, sent 50,000 outdated, unpopular books to a warehouse for storage. The landfill wouldn't accept them because, in Halifax, it's illegal to toss recyclables into the landfill. (The covers were garbage, but all the books' pages were recyclable.) The university decided it was too expensive to pay someone to rip off all the covers, so eventually they offered the books to anyone who wanted them.

In 2012, a builder called David Cameron asked for 10,000 of those books to be delivered to an old school a few hours away. Until then, no one had wanted the school either. All the students had moved to another school, and the building was abandoned. But Mr. Cameron and others wanted to turn it into a community center. Trouble was, the building had barely any insulation. But now, with stacks of books all along the walls (and more on the floor for added insulation), the Blockhouse School is toasty all winter long.

At the Blockhouse School Project in Nova Scotia, books stacked against the walls keep rooms toasty all winter long. TIM REEVES-HORTON

DON'T TOSS THAT TOOTHBRUSH!

The bristles are bent, and big globs of toothpaste have dried in between. What do you do with old toothbrushes? Toss them... or donate them to the local university to help construct a new building?

In 2013, kids in Brighton, the United Kingdom (UK), offered hundreds of used toothbrushes to an innovative project at the University of Brighton—the UK's first permanent building made entirely of garbage. But the "Waste House" doesn't look like junk, and that's exactly the point. The architects (BBM) wanted to show that trash can make useful and safe building materials. The house's walls are filled with 19,800 toothbrushes, 2,000 kilograms (2.2 tons) of denim sleeves and pant legs, 4,000 VHS video cassettes, 4,000 plastic DVD cases, and many other items that became insulation instead of landfill.

The toothbrushes of today can become the walls of tomorrow! UNIVERSITY OF BRIGHTON

The kitchen counter is made with washed-out coffee grounds and plastic coffee cups, and 500 bicycle inner tubes seal the windows and soundproof the floor. Usually, construction is hard on the environment because it uses up natural resources (like trees) and creates plenty of waste. But as the 253 students and apprentices who built this house have learned, construction can actually help save the environment, one worn-out toothbrush at a time.

MAKE IT A MAKER PARTY

Oops. You've leaned up against a freshly painted lamppost, and now your sleeve is dark green. Do you scream and kick the lamppost (covering your toes in green paint too)? Or do you do what teens in Chicago's One With Nature (OWN) club do and organize a Maker Party?

At Maker Parties, kids and teens learn how to turn old, worn or stained items into new fashions, jewelry or even furniture. They spend an afternoon with friends, learn new skills, get "new" stuff and don't have to pay a penny. Best of all, just one Maker Party can keep hundreds of pounds of trash out of the landfill.

How? Here's the deal. When we toss something away, we're not just throwing away a few pounds of trash. Manufacturing produces a lot of waste—often 40 times the weight of the actual product! For example, when factories make furniture, large parts of trees wind up as scrap too, and any packaging goes straight to the landfill. For every pound of trash that a household throws away, 40 pounds of trash were produced in making whatever was tossed. By making our own things and buying less, we stop waste before it's even created.

Victor and Jason are upcycling used T-shirts into laptop bags at this Maker Party.
DEBRA KERR/YOUTHMUSE

GARBAGE, BE GONE!

Since human beings first walked the Earth, we have invented creative solutions to our problems. These days, people are realizing that we create too much garbage, and the key to solving the waste problem is to change the way we live. What if everyone decided that, from now on, waste doesn't have to exist? Is that idea garbage or could it work? Dive into the next chapter to find out!

Old bottles can be turned into unique drinking glasses. This girl's family operates Artech Glass Blowing Studios in Ontario, Canada. ARTECHSTUDIOS.CA

Take in the Trash!

Pallets are wooden platforms used for shipping. Usually, once they've made their trip, they get tossed. But Ken Winchester and Jennifer McKimmie, who work hard to make their neighborhood store a community gathering place, saw the pallets as an opportunity. Now instead of taking up space in the landfill, the pallets offer a comfortable place to rest and a conversation topic for many passersby!

This furniture, made out of pallets, is the handiwork of Ken Winchester, co-owner of my favorite store, Niagara Grocery.
MICHELLE MULDER

CHAPTER FOUR

No Garbage Here

There's no doubt about what this man is protesting in Oregon.
TFOXFOTO/SHUTTERSTOCK.COM

STOP! IT'S THE PLASTIC POLICE!

Fighting crime, keeping the streets safe and protecting people from danger—that's what the police are for, right? In 2001, officials in Mumbai, India, realized that the city was flooding because plastic bags clogged the storm water drains in the streets. So the city made thin plastic bags illegal and created a special group of police officers to perform "plastic bag raids" in local markets. Anyone caught giving customers thin plastic bags had to pay a big fine (and, of course, the police took away all their bags too).

Governments around the world are banning plastic bags for all sorts of reasons. Some want to save the lives of birds and animals that might eat or get tangled in the plastic. Others worry about human health, forests, farmers' fields or beaches. And still others want to save all the energy and resources used to make plastic in the first place. Any way you look at it, though, something as simple as using a cloth bag makes a big difference to the planet.

POISON IN MY PLATE!?

Think of your favorite food. Maybe it's pizza with lots of melty cheese, or sushi with extra wasabi. Now picture your favorite food served on a toxic plate. Would you still eat it?

Polystyrene is a plastic product often used in disposable plates. It's cheap, which is why many institutions (like school cafeterias) like it. But polystyrene is known to contain *neurotoxicants*—chemicals that damage the brain. In 2008, the Young Activist Club at Piney Branch Elementary School (Takoma Park, Maryland) researched the problem, and they raised money to buy washable lunch trays, metal cutlery and a dishwasher. But when they asked school officials for permission to use the dishwasher for one year, the school board said washing plates was too expensive. Not willing to give up, the club organized petitions and trash-free lunch days, participated in festivals, spoke at public meetings and gave interviews to media all over the United States.

TRASH FACT: Every year, people use 500 billion to 1 trillion plastic shopping bags. Most aren't recycled and instead wind up in landfills, trees or waterways.

Students at Piney Branch Elementary School in Takoma Park, Maryland, want a school dishwasher to protect both the environment and their health. BRENDA PLATT, INSTITUTE FOR LOCAL SELF-RELIANCE

In 2014, school officials said they'd swap polystyrene lunch trays for cardboard ones throughout the district in 2015. The new trays will still be tossed into the local incinerator after one use, but at least kids won't be eating off dangerous plates anymore. The Young Activist Club continues to campaign for the right to use a dishwasher.

PLEASE FEED THE WORMS

Remember back in Chapter Two when all those food scraps in our landfills took ages to break down…and created dangerous gases in the meantime?

Many people keep food scraps out of their landfill by composting. Think about the microorganisms that munched up the food scraps of our caveman ancestors. Times may have changed, but microorganisms still love to chow down on vegetable scraps and turn them into moist, brown compost. (It takes about nine months to a year. Animal products take a little longer and need to be in a special animal-proof container so as not to attract rats and other scavengers.)

In some places, city workers pick up food scraps separately from other trash, compost them in a special facility and sell the product to farmers. Whether you do it yourself or your city does it for you, composting food scraps means less methane from landfills. In Canada, landfills create 20 percent of this harmful gas. Putting your apple core in the right bucket is an easy way to slow down climate change.

Compost…good for worms, good for gardening, and good for the planet.
CJP/ISTOCK.COM

GETTING YOUR FIX

Uh-oh, the toaster's broken. No one in your family knows how to fix it, and repair shops (if they even exist) don't fix them because it's cheaper to buy a new one. So now what?

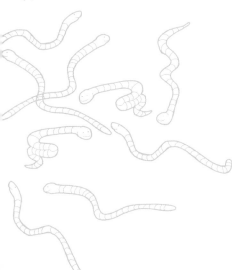

In 2009, Martine Postma organized the first Repair Café in Amsterdam, the Netherlands. She wanted to create a free meeting place where people could bring broken electrical appliances, furniture, clothes, bicycles, kitchenware, toys and other items from their houses and learn how to repair them. Soon, the idea began to spread, and now Repair Cafés exist in over a hundred cities around the world. Fewer things end up in the landfill, which means that fewer people buy new products. This saves them money and helps the environment too. And the Repair Cafés have another bonus as well: many of our best repair people are the elderly. At Repair Cafés, older people can offer their time and knowledge, and younger people get to learn new skills. Together, they build stronger communities.

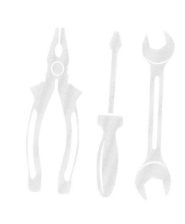

People fix everything from socks to circuit boards at Toronto's Repair Café. This audio equipment will soon be working again. CARMEN LIU, REPAIR CAFÉ TORONTO

GOOD NEIGHBORS

You found a funky chair at the side of the road. Your mom gave you a can of red paint, and all you need now is a paintbrush. You look everywhere. No luck. So do you head to the store? Of course not! Your next-door neighbor is much closer, and why buy something you'll only need for a few hours anyway? If you don't know any of your neighbors, check out Streetbank.com, a neighborhood-resource-sharing website that connects neighbors around the world.

Sam Stephens started Streetbank in London, England, in 2010. He already enjoyed a great relationship with his own neighbors. He'd borrowed small things at first—a cup of sugar here, a hedge-pruning set there—and eventually his neighbors became friends. Streetbank started as his way of letting people in his neighborhood know what they could borrow from each other. The website now serves more than 39,000 people around the world. He believes sharing makes people happier, and it also makes us less attached to our stuff. Best of all, it makes neighborhoods really feel like home.

A TRIP TO THE TRASH PALACE

Pink wallpaper with green swirls. An old door. An exercise machine. Seven hundred and three elastic bands. They're all cluttering up your garage, and there's no room left for your bicycle. Depending on where you live, you might pile everything by the side of the road with a sign that says *Free*. Or you could call a charity to come by and pick up the items for resale. Then again, maybe you live in Porirua, New Zealand, and the answer is obvious: take a trip to the Trash Palace.

The Trash Palace is one of many places around the world that collects reusable items people don't want. The Trash Palace has been open since 1996 and sells everything from doors to kettles. Workers collect almost anything that two people can carry

One person's junk is another's treasure at the Trash Palace in Porirua, New Zealand.
SIWILLIAMS.CO.NZ

into a truck. Money from their business supports people with mental illness. And once a month, people are welcome to come and grab all sorts of items for free. The Trash Palace is diverting so many objects from the landfill that it doesn't have room to store them all.

ZEROING IN ON ZERO WASTE

Porirua is one of many zero-waste communities in New Zealand. Zero-waste communities aim to create as little waste as possible. For some people that sounds like a silly goal—how could we possibly live without waste? But many believe that zero waste is the only goal we should have. After all, when we think about, say, driving safety on the roads, we aim for 100 percent. Why not aim for the best when it comes to our environment too?

People around the world have adopted the zero-waste lifestyle, aiming to reduce as much as possible the items they throw away. 29MOKARA/ISTOCK.COM

Take in the Trash!

My friends Chris and Susannah run an urban farm here in Victoria. They've got chickens, ducks, bees, fruit trees and rows and rows of vegetables. Friends and neighbors stop by regularly to admire the garden, chat, feed the chickens or dump vegetable scraps into one of several buckets that Chris set up along his fence. All these scraps turn into compost that keeps the vegetables coming up every month of the year.

Kitchen scraps from neighbors keep this garden lush and productive.
MICHELLE MULDER

Carter Schmidt's composting business turns his neighborhood's food scraps into a local resource. CARTERSCOMPOST.COM

Buying secondhand isn't just good for the environment—it can be a great way to meet people in your neighborhood too!
DAVID SACKS/THINKSTOCK.COM

You don't need to live in a zero-waste community to adopt a zero-waste lifestyle though. Here's how you can work toward it on your own:

Feed the Worms

Even if your city doesn't compost, your family can. Make space for a worm composter under the kitchen sink.

Buy Less (Reduce)

The less stuff we buy, the less trash we produce. Of course, we all need to buy some things (shelter, medicine and personal care products are necessary purchases), but sometimes we can borrow instead of buying. Also, sometimes we accept items we don't even want—like plastic bags—just because it's easier than saying no. Every "No" to unnecessary items is a "Yes!" to a clean and healthy planet.

Find It Secondhand

Seventy percent of people on our planet wear secondhand clothing. But for many of the other 30 percent, wearing used clothing is like wearing a big sign that says *I'm Poor*. What if we change that way of thinking? Buying secondhand saves people money, but even better, it gives new life to something that might otherwise be thrown away, and it saves the energy and resources needed to make new clothing. Besides, people who buy secondhand are much more empowered to experiment with their clothing. With a little dye, fabric paint or creative sewing, secondhand can be truly sensational!

Tell 'Em What You Think

Have you ever heard the expression "Money talks"? When we spend money on one product instead of another, we're giving manufacturers important information. The more we spend on long-lasting items without much packaging, for example, the harder manufacturers will try to produce such items. Writing letters or emails to manufacturers is another great way to tell them what's important to you.

Fix It

Lots of things can be fixed with a little creative thinking. And grandparents or elderly neighbors—or anyone who's used to getting by with less—are often happy to help with the fixing. That broken bike isn't a pile of trash. It's a community project and terrific future transportation!

Make It Yourself

A carrot fresh from the ground doesn't have a scrap of packaging on it. Growing our own food is a fun and delicious way to make less waste. And do-it-yourself doesn't have to stop there. Why not try your hand at making your own clothes, bread, greeting cards and gifts?

What's better than riding a bicycle? Knowing how to fix (or build) your own!
JUPITERIMAGES.COM

Food tastes even better when you've grown it yourself. LUCIDIO STUDIO INC/GETTY.COM

Every year, on April 30, kids gather in Vondelpark, Amsterdam, the Netherlands, to sell their used clothes, toys and books. VLIET/ISTOCK.COM

Give It a New Life

And if it's not broken, but you're tired of it, why not pass it on? The more used items available in a community, the fewer new ones we need to produce.

A FRESH, FRAGRANT FUTURE, ANYONE?

When there's not much money to go around, people get creative to make ends meet. We grow our own vegetables, ride bikes more, and use old jars to store food instead of buying fancy containers. We also share more, and we make whatever we have last longer. And these habits aren't just good for the planet—they're good for communities too.

People are natural problem solvers. From composting to clever clothing creations to community work parties, we've got all the resources and skills we need to keep our planet healthy and trash-free, just like nature intended. Zero waste, here we come!

These days, more and more cities are composting. This is the compost symbol used in Marin County, California.
ZEROWASTEMARIN.ORG

Take in the Trash!

A few years ago, my friend Mireille gave me a hand-made journal that she created after a particularly successful Dumpster dive. A stack of dot-matrix printer paper (only useful for really, really old printers) became the pages. The covers of old hardcover books became covers for a new one. Magazine cutouts decorated the outside, and the binding came from some old twine she'd found on her dive too. The book is one of the most beautiful gifts I've ever received.

My favorite notebook is made entirely from Dumpster finds. MICHELLE MULDER

Resources

Books

McKay, Kim, and Jenny Bonnin. *True Green Kids: 100 Things You Can Do to Save the Planet.* Washington, DC: National Geographic, 2008.

Movies

Amarilla, Alejandra, and Juliana Penaranda-Loftus. *Landfill Harmonic.* Meeta Productions, Hidden Village Films and Eureka Productions, 2015.

Leonard, Annie, and Jonah Sachs. *The Story of Solutions.* Free Range Studios, 2013. http://storyofstuff.org/movies/the-story-of-solutions/.

Websites

Carter's Compost: www.carterscompost.com
The Freecycle Network: www.freecycle.org
Repair Café: www.repaircafe.org
Streetbank: www.streetbank.com
Two Hands Project: www.twohandsproject.com
The Waste House: www.viralnova.com/trash-house/2
Young Activist Club: www.youngactivistclub.org

Acknowledgments

In the year that I've been working on this book, many friends have been alarmed when I told them what I was writing was "garbage." Thank you for the hugs and support when you thought I was just being too hard on myself!

Many thanks, too, to friends who offered stories for this book: Andrew Mott, Paul Holt, Drew Tupper, Mark Weston, Mireille Evans, Sarah Harvey, Catherine Vandermeulen, Binnie Brennan, Kari Jones, and Chris and Susannah Adams. Several books for adults helped me better understand my subject. Among my favorites have been *The Story of Stuff* by Annie Leonard with Ariane Conrad, *Zero Waste Home* by Bea Johnson, and *The Zero Waste Solution* by Paul Connett. I'd also like to thank the many people who offered information or photos for *Trash Talk*, including Brenda Platt and Nadine Bloch (parent volunteers of the Young Activist Club), Jennifer McKimmie and Ken Winchester of Niagara Grocery, Thomas LeCourt and Jason Adams of reFUSE Resource Recovery.

I'd especially like to thank my excellent friend Susan Braley for the listening ear, laughter, thoughtfulness and generosity that helped make *Trash Talk* possible. Thank you to the BC Arts Council for providing the financial assistance that allowed me to write it, and thanks to Orca Book Publishers—particularly Sarah Harvey, Naomi Lee and Jenn Playford—for turning my words into a gorgeous book.

And finally, thanks to my family for cheering me on as I wrote, and for sharing my excitement when I find furniture, pickle jars, books, plants, planters, tea and all other manner of things on the street and bring them home. (And three cheers for Maia, who loves a good free pile just as much as I do!) Thank you, everyone.

Who says plastic bottles are only for beverages? PHONLAWAT_778/DREAMSTIME.COM

Index

*Page numbers in **bold** indicate an image; there may also be text related to the same topic on that page*

Index (continued)